Machine Learning Guide:

A Practical Approach for Businesses

Table of Contents

Introduction

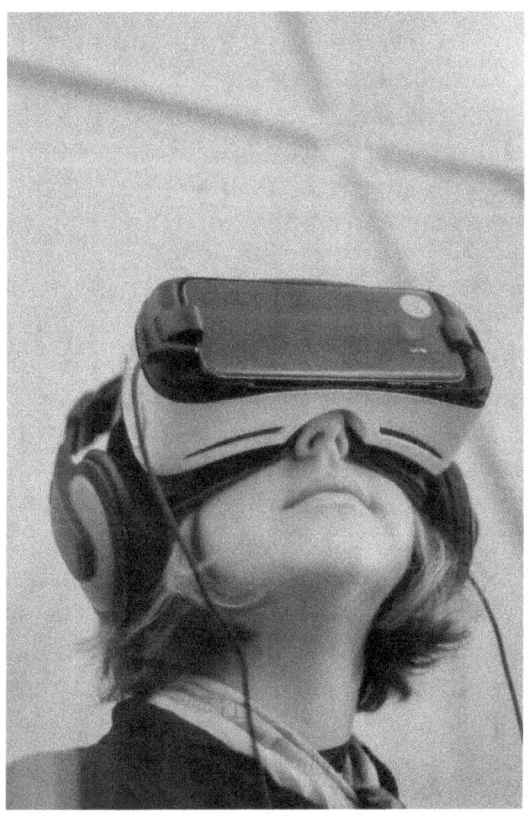

Photo by <u>Samuel Zeller</u> on <u>Unsplash</u>

Congratulations and thank you for downloading *Machine Learning Guide: A Practical Approach for Businesses*. The following chapters will discuss the application of machine learning in the twenty-first century, methods of machine learning, how it is applicable in the current age and what some of its current uses are put toward, the importance of data in relation to machine learning, popular algorithms, and how you can apply all of those things toward your business to make it run smoother and more efficient.

What is machine learning? Machine learning is considered a subset of artificial intelligence; it is a method of analyzing data in order to automate analytical model building. Machine learning has its basis on the concept that a system may teach itself to learn from provided data so that the machine can make its own decisions, learn from said data, and identify patterns with little to no human supervision. While this phenomenon comes naturally to humans and some animals, computational methods allow machines to "learn" directly from the data without having to rely on a predetermined equation. As you give the algorithms more and more samples, they begin to adaptively improve their performances. A machine learning model has three parts: the parameters, the model, and a learner.

A model is the conclusion you are trying to reach like the thesis statement in an essay. As the system analyzes data, the model learns from the data you give it. Unlike a thesis statement, the model doesn't have to be backed by any facts, credible or not, as long as the model gives the system a frame of reference as to what you are looking to understand from the data. Parameters in terms of machine learning are what is being assessed: the factors and the data being analyzed. These parameters will never change so they act as concrete guidelines as to what information the system should focus on. Lastly, the learner is the system that the machine used to analyze and understand the data in relation to the model, and then it tweaks that model to match the new information.

Machine learning has many advantages over humans due to the large amounts of data they can process at one time and how fast they can perform complex equations. This capacity put into a business context has the potential to be powerful and productive. A system that, when fed raw data, can analyze and crunch the numbers for you will increase productivity and save you time.

There are plenty of books on this subject on the market, so thanks again for choosing this one! Every effort was made to ensure it is full of as much useful information as possible. Please enjoy!

Chapter 1: Machine Learning in Today's World

Photo by <u>Franck V.</u> on <u>Unsplash</u>

To see results from machine learning, you need to pair an algorithm with the right tools and processes to get the values you are looking for. We will discuss these algorithms in later chapters more in-depth, but they include decision trees, neural networks, associations and sequence discoveries, random forests, support vector machines, gradient boosting, k-means clustering, nearest-neighbor mapping, and self-organizing maps among many others. But results are not based completely on the algorithms: the value resides in the pairing of your data with an algorithm best-suited for the task you want to complete. Many industries out there deal with large amounts of data and some companies have realized that there is value in using this kind of technology to assist in the sorting and interpretation of all of that data.

Companies involved in finances use machine learning technology for identifying key insights in data and for preventing fraudulent activities from happening to their customers. These insights can pinpoint potential investment opportunities or even help an investor know when the right time to trade their stocks may be. Data mining—examining large databases to generate new information—can help financial institutions identify clients that are at a higher risk to be targeted, or incorporate it into cyber-surveillance to alert them to warning signs of fraud taking place. Across the government, agencies like public safety and utilities have a gold mine of data from multiple sources that can be tapped into to provide a wealth of insights. Wearable technology that uses sensors collects data and allows healthcare professionals to access a patient's health in real time and identify red flags and trends which can lead the patient to experience better overall health and even receive improved diagnoses and treatments.

Have you noticed that after browsing through websites, similar items begin to pop up in ads on your current webpage? Marketers use machine learning to recommend items you may like based on previous purchases and sites you have already looked at to analyze your buying history and suggest new purchases. Online shopping experiences can be very tailored and personalized, and marketers can capitalize on that by using all of this information during the formation of new marketing campaigns. Oil and gas distributors tap into this technology to help them find new energy sources, analyze minerals at a new potential location, and predict when a sensor on machinery may fail. Machine learning has made the distribution of oil and gas more streamlined, efficient, and cost-effective for their companies. Lastly, the transportation industry uses data to predict and identify patterns and trends regarding traffic routes, and the information can also be used to make routes faster and more effective for companies in all kinds of sectors such as delivery companies and public transportation like the city bus or UBER drivers.

Other industries that could benefit from machine learning include image processing and computer vision, computational biology, natural language processing, and automotive, aerospace, and manufacturing companies. When should you tap into machine learning for your business? It is when you have a complex task at hand that involves a large amount of data, a large number of variables, and there is no existing formula or equation for computation. Machine learning employs two different techniques to make it work: supervised and unsupervised learning. Reinforcement learning and semi-supervised learning are also used, but a more in-depth analysis of those methods will be discussed further in Chapter 2. Supervised learning trains a machine learning model on known input and output values so that it can come up with a future prediction for those outputs using a system of classification or regression, while unsupervised learning is modeled on finding hiding patterns or intrinsic structures in the data you program into it using clustering.

While directly related to machine learning, artificial intelligence encompasses both that and deep learning—so, what is the difference between them you ask? Coined in 1956, the term artificial intelligence has come to describe a machine that can perform tasks that are characteristically human and at the same intelligence level. Planning, language comprehension, object and sound recognition, learning, and problem-solving are all involved and artificial intelligence can be broken down into two categories: general and narrow. General artificial intelligence has all of the characteristics of a human, while narrow artificial intelligence lacks in some of the above-mentioned areas. Simply put, machine learning is a way of achieving artificial intelligence. Artificial intelligence can be achieved without using machine learning, but it would be much more difficult because it would require building line after line of code with complex rules and decision trees involved.

To bypass all of that work, machine learning can train an algorithm to learn hard coding software routines with specific instructions that allow it to accomplish a task. This training involves giving the algorithm large amounts of data and then letting the algorithm self-adjust to improve. Deep learning is one of several approaches to machine learning, and was inspired by the structure and function of the brain—namely its many interconnected neurons. Arterial Neural Networks (ANN), sometimes referred to as just neural networks, are algorithms programmed to mimic the human brain. Each neuron later learns a specific feature that creates depths and connections to other "neurons." The goal of machine learning is to understand and give meaning and context to the data you give it in order for that data to be put inside a model that can be understood and analyzed by other people.

As stated in The Harvard Business Review's article, "the most important thing to understand about ML is that it represents a fundamentally different approach to creating software: The machine learns from examples rather than being explicitly programmed for a particular outcome. This is an important break from previous practice." In the past, applications have only been able to advance to the point of having existing knowledge codified and placed into machines.

"Indeed, the term 'coding' denotes the painstaking process of transferring knowledge from developers' heads into a form that machines can understand and execute. This approach has a fundamental weakness: Much of the knowledge we all have is tacit, meaning that we can't fully explain it. It's nearly impossible for us to write down instructions that would enable another person to learn how to ride a bike or to recognize a friend's face."

Supervised learning systems have taken off in recent years, but any system can be successful when their training data contains thousands up to millions of examples from which they may learn from. Each example has the correct answer labeled on them, allowing the system to branch out and look at new information so that the training will lead the system to predict very accurate answers. Here are some examples of machine learning from The Harvard Business Review that involve mapping inputs to outputs:

INPUT X	OUTPUT Y	APPLICATION
Voice recording	Transcript	Speech recognition
Historical market data	Future market data	Trading bots
Photograph	Caption	Image tagging
Drug chemical properties	Treatment efficacy	Pharma R&D
Store transaction details	Is the transaction fraudulent?	Fraud detection
Recipe ingredients	Customer reviews	Food recommendations
Purchase histories	Future purchase behavior	Customer retention
Car locations and speed	Traffic flow	Traffic lights
Faces	Names	Face recognition

Deep learning is the neural network driver behind many of the algorithms successes. Deep learning has several advantages including their ability to better handle much larger sets of data. Older systems could take data up to a point, but after that point, additional data made no difference on the bettering the system's predictions. In the end, more data leads to better predictions just like continuing to practice a skill will make you better and better at that skill.

"It's comparatively straightforward to label a body of data and use it to train a supervised learner; that's why supervised ML systems are more common than unsupervised ones, at least for now. Unsupervised learning systems seek to learn on their own.

"We humans are excellent unsupervised learners: We pick up most of our knowledge of the world (such as how to recognize a tree) with little or no labeled data. But it is exceedingly difficult to develop a successful machine learning system that works this way."

Unsupervised learning has a lot of exciting potential for the future in the ways we can apply its functionality. These systems attempt to learn by themselves, unlike us as humans that thrive off of picking up on the knowledge of the world from little or no labeled data. Using an unsupervised system to analyze more complex problems so we can discover new patterns and solutions can be used from anything like predicting the spread of a particular disease to price moving across trading markets.

Another growing area is reinforcement learning, which is helping us optimize data center power usage among many others. "In reinforcement learning systems, the programmer specifies the current state of the system and the goal, lists allowable actions, and describes the elements of the environment that constrain the outcomes for each of those actions. Using the allowable actions, the system has to figure out how to get as close to the goal as possible. These systems work well when humans can specify the goal but not necessarily how to get there." The thing you've got to watch when using reinforced learning is the system's attempts to maximize the correct outputs on the basis of the rules it was designed to abide by; meaning, a reinforced system will strive for the goal that it is rewarded for computing, not necessarily the answer you are wanting to find out.

Machine learning is simple but is far-reaching in depth of knowledge and possibilities. With this growing second wave of technological advancements, new risks and limits are emerging, including how machine learning systems sometimes have a lower "interpretability," or difficulty understanding how the system reached that answer. Deep neural networks sometimes contain anywhere between hundreds to millions of different neural connections. Each of them has their own contributions to the final conclusion, usually leading to a difficult, unclear explanation. They can give us answers, but they still cannot tell us why—or in other words, machines know more than they are capable of telling us at this time.

While that's a good thing in one way, this inability to tell us how they got to an answer creates three risks. The first of the risks is the room for hidden biases in the machines that were not directly inputted by a designer into the system but biases that can form based on the data you used for training the system. As an example, if a system uses a past recruiter's choices regarding who got a job and who did not, the system could learn to perpetuate that recruiter's biases regarding race, gender, or others. What's worse is that the biases exist in the underlying interactions between the thousands of factors taken into consideration and may not even appear as an explicit rule.

The second risk, unlike a traditional system creates around strict logical rules, a neural network system handles statistical truths instead of any literal truths. This makes it almost impossible—or at the least very difficult—to have the system with absolute certainty prove that the solution will work in each and every case. This is especially in a situation where they were given no similar data to train on. Some systems need decisions made with absolute certainties, like a nuclear power plant control, so this lack of verifiability is concerning.

Third, if the machine learning system makes an error, as it likely will, finding the cause of the problem can be a challenge. You have to find the underlying structure that allowed the system to find the solution which can be complex, and that solution might not be optimal under the conditions of which it was trained to change. All three of these are very real risks, and in certain cases, the outcome may not be perfection, but an alternative that is the best of what's available. Like humans, machines make mistakes, have biases, and can sometimes struggle to explain the truth behind our arrival at its chosen answer. The advantages here is that, over time, a machine learning system can improve and continue to give the same answers when given the same data.

Chapter 2: Machine Learning Methods

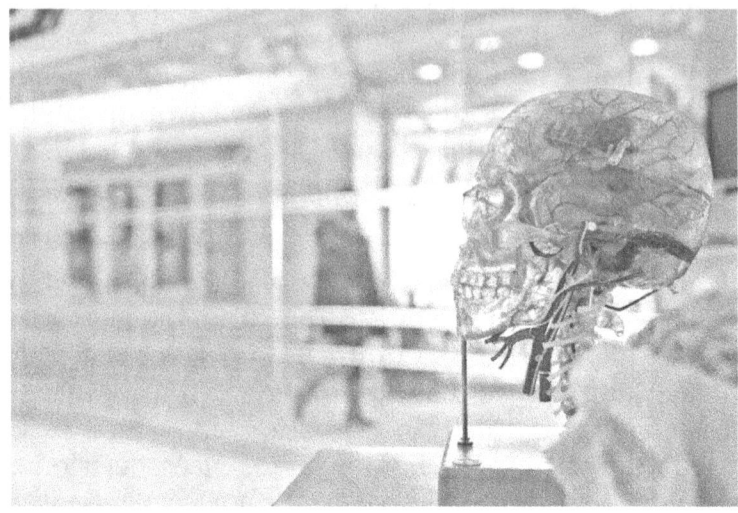

Photo by Jesse Orrico on Unsplash

We briefly touched on methods of machine learning in the previous chapter, but now we will look more in-depth into these methods and how they work. Supervised machine learning builds a model that takes into consideration the presence of uncertainty to make predictions based on hard evidence. An algorithm using this method trains the model to generate reasonable predictions depending on the data you are continually inputting. A common use for this model is to take historical data and analyze it to statistically predict the likelihood of certain events occurring. An example of supervised learning would be the use of "tagging" on Facebook. When you post a new photo Facebook will ask you if you would like to tag anyone in the photo. The next time you go to post, Facebook may have already identified the faces in the photo for you to click on and tag, or the site may even suggest who you should tag based on previous photos you have uploaded.

Neural networks are only one of several types of machine learning models that were being used for the past half-century. The node is the most important unit of a neural network, and this node is very loosely based on the actual neurons found in the human brain. The nodes are connected, and these connections, similar to the brain, develop over time through practice, or "training."

Deep learning is behind the success of the algorithms, and it uses these neural networks. The algorithms behind deep learning have an advantage on older versions of machine learning algorithms because of their ability to use a much larger set of data. Old machine learning algorithms could continue to improve up to a point as more examples were added to the training data, but after that point, putting in new data did not continue to lead to better predictions from the system. For some unknown reason, deep neural networks do not seem to level out in the same way. For deep neural networks the more data you give it, the better predictions you get.

Deep learning has neural networks with many layers and parameters in one of four fundamentals architecture networks:

- Convolutional neural networks

- Unsupervised pre-trained networks

- Recursive neural networks

- Recurrent neural networks

If you are a visual learner, picture the relationship between machine learning, artificial intelligence, and deep learning as the following: the area of artificial intelligence encompasses the field of machine learning, and inside the field of machine learning you can find deep learning. What differentiates deep learning networks in general from data-forward multilayer networks are the existence of more neurons that are on previous networks, an explosion of computing power to rain, more complicated ways of connecting layers, and an automatic feature extraction.

Any time that you have a large amount of data on a behavior and the answer you want to predict could potentially be applied to a supervised learning system. The filtering algorithms based on memory that have been used in the past have largely been replaced by these systems in order to make the recommendation process more personalized. It's quite easy to label a data set and then use it in a system to train a supervised learning system.

Supervised learning uses two kinds of techniques: classification and regression. Classification techniques predict discrete responses by classifying data input into the system into categories. For example, determining whether an email is legitimate or spam is based on the technique, or computing your credit score. Techniques used include support vector machines, discriminant analysis, naïve Bayes, and nearest neighbor. Regression techniques predict continuous answers like the ongoing tracking of weather patterns and how that effects AC demands in the summer and heat demands in the winter. Supervised learning is great for making predictions, while unsupervised learning is better equipped to help you navigate the data you have to create a model that will represent the data well. Techniques for regression include linear regression/GLM, SVR/GPR, ensemble methods, decision trees, and neural networks.

Unsupervised learning uses unlabeled data that forces the learning algorithm to find commonalities among the data on its own. This data is more abundant and commonly used for transactional data. You don't tell the machine the "right" answer so that the unsupervised learning methods can look at all of the data and potentially organize it in a meaningful way. One area this technique is used in is for determining fraudulent credit and debit card purchases. If the system can tell you usually don't spend over $50 on your credit card at one time but detects a transaction for $200 it may flag it as a purchase you did not make. The technique used for this kind of learning is called clustering, and it does that through several means: k-means, hierarchical, Gaussian Mixture, neural networks, or the Hidden Markov Model.

There is also a small but continually expanding area within the machine learning field called reinforcement learning. In systems like the Atari video game, this learning approach is embedded and able to optimize the power usage and create trading plans surrounding the stock market. A real-life example is Kindred's use of robots that use machine learning to find and sort objections they have never come into contact with before, therefore speeding up the process of choosing and placing in consumer goods distribution centers. Programmers who use the reinforcement learning system get to choose the state of the system and the desired outcome, list allowable actions, and tell the user what elements of the environment that shape the possible outcomes for each listed action. The benefit of this system is that if the user specifies the goal but does not give much instruction on how to get there, the system focuses on the allowable actions to figure out how to get as close to the outcome as it can. The downside of this system can be seen in its optimization for the desired outcome because it is the only one you explicitly reward, even though that may be different from what you actually care about.

Chapter 3: Applications for Machine Learning and Artificial Intelligence

How can you incorporate machine learning into your everyday life? We are going to touch on a handful of fields where the application of machine learning is widely used or an up-and-coming development. Let's first take a look at security—in particular, cybersecurity. In the cybersecurity world, we want to harness the power of machine learning to find differences: in this case, malicious behavior that comes in the form of hackers, malware, ransomware, etc. The only problem with defining these differences is that to determine what is different, you must determine what is normal. There are always exceptions to the rule as well, so configuring a system that can help you better analyze potential threats and respond to these attacks can be a great benefit to a business. Machine learning automates these complex processes that the system uses to detect attacks and react to security breaches. The integration of this technology will need to be done together with both man (analysts) and machine (the system).

We are going to include fraud prevention with cybersecurity as they generally fall under the same umbrella of issues. As with any technology, as the technology evolves, so do the threats. Attackers have been able to become more sophisticated in how they determine vulnerabilities and how with how large of an attack they can coordinate. Machine learning can allow a system to identify and prevent fraud in a variety of retail markets online. Some of the applications of machine learning in fraud prevention range from validating users when opening an account to authorizing payments. Speaking of money, the field of finance has greatly benefitted from machine learning because a lot of what they both do is similar: handle high volumes and accurate records, help companies do everything from approving loans to manage assets to assessing risks.

The stock market has changed dramatically over the last several decades, thanks to machine learning. Stock markets have become more dynamic, with high-frequency trades replacing more traditional exchange-based trading. The market generates a massive amount of data from many sources like economic reports and financial reports. You can now find commission-free stock brokerage platforms that capture a wider market by creating new algorithmic trading systems to help those that may never otherwise traded due to money constraints or lack of knowledge. These systems have made trading so easy that large hedge funds and individual investors just beginning to trade.

Healthcare could use a push past the digitalization of medical records and begin exploring how they can use machine learning and analytics to provide better information to healthcare providers. While a doctor is with a patient, it is of utmost importance that the information they have is correct and as up-to-date as possible. Giving the doctor quick and easy access to say, a patient's risk of a stroke or kidney failure based on the collected and analyzed numbers gathered straight from the patient themselves, will allow doctors to have this kind of information at their fingertips will lead to better decisions regarding patient diagnoses, treatment options, and possible outcomes, leading to overall better care. There are many sectors within the healthcare field that have large image databases like radiology, cardiology, and pathology. As we know, machine learning can train a system to look at images, identify differences, and point to areas needing improvement, over time, ensuring the accuracy of the model. The more data added to the model over time will allow doctors to have better predictive capabilities to diagnose, educate, and treat patients, therefore leading to a healthier community.

All companies, particularly the larger ones with a national or global presence, employ marketing to get the word out about their organization and available products and services. Marketers have already been incorporating machine learning to understand and anticipate consumer trends, which have led them to grow their revenue and better understand their customers to increase future satisfaction with the company. The future of marketing and machine learning will hope to shape and mold models to improve customer experiences and support, personalize customer care and cross-channel advertising, develop new products, ensure message targeting accuracy, price optimizing, forecasting, creating a model that can cross-sell and up-sell products, generate leads, and identifying and defining sales projections.

Google, one of the most-used search engines, has already been using machine learning for refining the search features they currently have like relying less on content quality as a ranking factor and focusing more on updating their algorithms to better determine the quality of its content. An update they have made within the last five years includes RankBrain, a system improvement that allows the search engine to look at the phrase of a search instead of just analyzing the words; in effect, the system can tell the meaning behind your search instead of only dissecting the search and pulling up sites that had some or all of the keywords. RankBrain has also allowed Google to tie together similar queries which would teach the system to associate commonalities between all the questions revolving around the same topic.

Natural Language Processing (NLP) is part of artificial intelligence that involves the analysis of written language. NPL can take a lot of data in the form of plain text and give the system insights like sentiment analysis, information extraction, information retrieval, etc. Machine learning aims to study and develop NLP systems that an interpret speech and text as people naturally talk and type. The human language is very complex with colloquialisms, abbreviations, slang, and all sorts of misspellings. Machine learning can recognize overall sentences but struggle to find exact themes and topic similarities, but it struggles to refer those back to individual themes. Improvements to the model over the years include language modeling, text classification, caption generation, speech recognition, document summarization, machine translation, and question answering.

Lastly, the growing concept of self-driving cars has come alive during the 21st century. Advanced and complex, self-driving cars need to understand the rules of the road, how to drive, how to monitor the movements and signals of other cars on the road, how the road infrastructure works, and how to negotiate exceptions and make rapid decisions in the moment. Many road accidents are caused by human error, so the thought is that by using self-driving cars, we can greatly reduce the number of accidents. Companies have been experimenting with these kinds of cars, but there are still concerns about the cars being able to navigate unexpected events, exceptions, and ethical situations. Subaru, for example, has added automatic emergency braking systems to their new models in the hopes that this technology will save lives over the years. Other uses for machine learning in cars can be seen in the data the car generates that can continually indicate how efficiently the vehicle is operating and how much the driver is using the vehicle and integrating the internet and personal smart devices with the car.

Chapter 4: Collecting Data to Train a Machine Learning Model

Photo by Tirza van Dijk on Unsplash

In this chapter, we are going to walk through the steps it would take to create a system that can analyze data and provide you an answer to a question. This system that will find an answer is the model, and the model will be created via training to make a model that correctly answers our questions a majority of the time. The systems train itself using the data you feed it. Now, let's look at the first step which is gathering data.

Let's say that we want to create a system that answers the question of whether a drink is water or soda. The data for the system will be collected from the photos, and while there are many aspects of the drinks we can focus on, for the sake of this example, we will focus on the color and fizz content. The first step in the process of creating a system is to gather the data. We want quality data and as much of it as we can get. This data will directly determine how good your machine learning model can be. In the case of our example, we will collect data on the color and bubble content of each drink.

The next step is data preparation where we will enter the data gathered into a system to prepare it first to use in our machine learning training. The order of the system's learning does not depend on whether the drink is soda or water, so we want to randomize the order of the data we enter. You want the data entered to have equal representations of both so that the system does not become biased toward guessing that everything it sees is water if all the data you entered is about the water. The second part of data preparation is the separation of data into two parts: the first part of the data we will use in our training model, and this will encompass a majority of the data collected. The rest of the data we will use later in order to determine if the trained model met our performance standards. The data needs to be split up this way the because if we used the same data for evaluation as we did on the model, the model would remember the questions in the same way that your math teacher may pull some of the test questions from the homework they assign. The last part of data preparation is the adjusting and manipulating of the data for normalization and error correction among others.

All of this data will be inputted into a model, so our next step to creating a system is choosing the right model to use. There are many models out there, each suited to something different like image data, sequence data, or numerical data. For this example, we have only the two features: color and fizz content. A smaller, simpler, linear model should do the trick in this case. Next comes the training of the model. We will use the gathered data to improve the model's ability over time to predict whether a drink is water or soda. Since we are using a linear model, we will use the formula $y=mx+b$ where "y" is the output, "m" is the slope, "x" is the input, and "b" is the y-intercept. The training values will be input into "m" and "b" and there will be a lot of "m" values since there are many features in machine learning. The collection of this data can be formed into a matrix which can help visualize and organize your data. Some random values for "w" and "b" will be required in the beginning so the system can start training to begin predicting what the output of those values will be. Weights and biases can be compared with the model's predictions with the output it produced, and then the values can be adjusted to produce more correct predictions in future training. We started with a random line through the data, but during each training step, the line moves closer to an ideal separation between the water and soda.

Evaluation is the next step to determine if the model is useful. This is where we take the other part of the data that we set aside earlier so we can test the model against that data that has never been used for training purposes. This testing will let you see how the model would work in the real world if you choose to use it. If you don't like the way the model is working, you can tune the parameters by shifting the line during training steps. While our linear model is simple, when using a more complex model, the initial conditions can greatly impact the role in how the outcome of the training is determined. You must define what you consider to make the model good enough or you will spend a long time continuing to tweak the parameters.

How is a prediction determined? Machine learning in its essence is using the data to answer your questions. At this point in time, we can actually use the model to predict whether a drink is water or soda given its color and fizz percentage. The big picture from all of this gathering and plugging and predicting will leave us with a model that will be able to determine between water and soda, without relying on human judgment and rules.

Chapter 5: Artificial Intelligence and Machine Learning Algorithms

Photo by Markus Spiske on Unsplash

As we discussed in Chapter 2, there are three types of machine learning algorithms: supervised learning, unsupervised learning, and reinforcement learning.

Supervised learning algorithms:

- Linear Regression
- Decision Tree
- Random Forest
- KNN
- Logistic Regression
- Support Vector Machine (SVM)
- Naïve Bayes
- Dimensionality Reduction
- Boosting

Unsupervised learning algorithms:

- Apriori
- K-means clustering

Reinforcement learning algorithms

These are only a small example of supervised learning, unsupervised learning, and reinforcement learning algorithms. Let's explore these algorithms more in-depth and learn what the algorithms are used for with real-world examples.

Linear Regression

This algorithm is built to estimate real values based on on-going variables. These real values can be anything from the cost of a car to a number of emails received. A relationship between an independent and a dependent variable by finding a single line that best fits all of the data. This line is called the regression line and is represented by the algebraic expression $y = ax + b$. y is the dependent variable, a is the slope, x is the independent variable, and b is the intercept. The variables a and b are found by squaring the difference of distance between data points and the regression line and then minimizing the sum. The linear regression algorithm comes in two types: *simple linear* which is characterized by one independent variable and *multiple linear* which is characterized by more than one independent variable.

Decision Tree

Commonly used for classification problems, the Decision Tree algorithm works both for categorical and continuous dependent variables. By splitting the population into two or more of the same sets, you can ensure the sets are homogenous based on the most important characteristics/independent variables. This algorithm is one of the best and most used machine learning methods with high certainty, stability, and the data is easy to interpret. The algorithm can segregate based on important values you select which in turn creates these sets of similar data. There are two types of decision trees: categorical variable decision trees and continuous variable decision trees. Decision trees are fast ways to identify variables that are significant to you and what the relationship between said variables is when referring to the algorithm.

Random Forest

The Random Forest algorithm is also used often because of its simplicity and because it can be used for classification and regression tasks. Using a group of decision trees, the algorithms employ a combination of learning models to increase the overall success of the results. Put simply, let's say you chose two features you wanted your machine learning system to focus on. This algorithm would split the data into two, and in each set, it would use different decision trees to come to a single answer which you can then compare the answer of the second data set. This process can create very diverse results due to the algorithm's search for the best feature while node splitting. These nodes are "tests" on a chosen attribute, the branches are the different outcomes available, and the leaf nodes stand for class labels (a leaf is a node with no children). Parameters can be set to increase the predictive power of the model or enable it to learn quicker.

k- Nearest Neighbor (KNN)

Also available to use for both classification and regression purposes, KNN keeps all available cases in its memory and is able to classify each new case by a majority vote of its k neighbors. A real-life example of this algorithm working would computing credit scores by analyzing all of the data on people's financial characteristics and compare it to others who have similar financial characteristics. We can see this in action when people who have similar financial characteristics have similar credit scores. This algorithm is non-parametric, meaning that it does not assume anything based on the underlying data distribution you provide the model. According to Medium.com, "KNN is also a lazy algorithm (as opposed to an *eager* algorithm).... What this means is that it does not use the training data points to do any *generalization*. In other words, there is *no explicit training phase* or it is very minimal. This also means that the training phase is pretty fast. Lack of generalization means that KNN keeps all the training data. To be more exact, all (or most) the training data is needed during the testing phase."

Logistic Regression

While the word regression is in the title, the logistic regression algorithm is actually used for classification purposes. Used to estimate discrete values of a given set of independent variables like yes/no or true/false, the model can predict the probability of an event happening by fitting data into a logit function. What is a logit you ask? A logit is a function of raw predictions generated by a classification model that shows you probability outcomes. For example, let's say you are playing a game of Monopoly. You have two outcomes: either you win the game, or you lose the game. Now let's say you are playing Monopoly and Clue and Sorry! in an attempt to find out which game you are best at. The outcome would be that given the circumstances you are 75% likely to win a game of Clue, but only 25% likely to win a game of Monopoly. This algorithm uses an equation to represent the data, much like linear regression. Input values, "X" combine linearly with coefficient values to predict outputs, "Y".

Support Vector Machine (SVM)

Using the SVM method, you are able to formally define a classifier by a hyperplane that separates the data into two sets using the given labeled training data. This algorithm is able to find a hyperplane that separates the classes. The line that separates the data can then be used to make classification by putting input values into the line equation you are able to determine whether a given point is above or below the line. A point above the line has a value greater than 0 making the point belong to class 0, a point below the line has a value of less than 0 and the point belongs to class 1, and a point close to the line has a value close to 0 meaning the point might be hard to classify. If you get a large value that means that your model has more confidence in its prediction. The margin of the distance between the line and the data point that resides the closest to it is the best line to separate the two groups of data.

Naïve Bayes

Based on an assumption that predictors are independent, the Naïve Bayes algorithm is another classification technique. It gets its roots from the Bayes' Theorem and has classifiers that assume the presence of a particular feature in a class that is not relevant to the presence of any other feature. For example, to consider a fruit to be an orange it has to be orange, round, and about 4 inches in diameter. Whether or not these features depend on each other or other features, each feature on its own contributes to the probability that that fruit is an orange. Great for large data sets, the Naïve Bayes algorithm is simple and provides a way to calculate posterior probability.

Dimensionality Reduction

Too many variables upon the basis of which the final classification is done is common in machine learning, and the higher the number of features there are, the harder it gets to see the training set and then modify it. Sometimes correlated and sometimes not, this process can reduce the number of random features you are looking at by using a set of principal values that get divided into a feature selection and feature extraction. The feature selection component attempts to find a subset in the original variable set that can find a smaller subset upon which to show the problem. This can be done one of three ways: filter, wrapper, and embedded. The feature extraction component minimizes the data in a high-dimensional space to a space with fewer or no dimensions.

Boosting

Boosting is a technique where predictors are made sequentially, not independently. This algorithm uses the logic where new predictors learn from the mistakes of old predictors. You can choose from a range of predictors, but you must set careful boundaries as to what your criteria are otherwise you may over-fit data training.

Apriori

The apriori algorithm can be used to mine frequent sets from a bottoms-up approach in an attempt to operate on database records. Able to take a larger set of data, the apriori algorithm "scores" it by comparing it in some way to other data sets that are ordered similarly. The calculated scores can then lead to sets that are labeled as frequent appearances in larger data sets for an accumulated data collection. An idea of how this algorithm works can be seen in an application like a financial analysis tool that is able to score how various stocks would trend together.

K-means clustering

This type of clustering is our first example of unsupervised learning, which as a refresher, is when you use unlabeled data (data that you have not defined into categories or groups), with the number of groups that represent the variable "K". The k-means algorithm assigns single data points to a K group based on variables provided. Clustered data points have similar variables, and the results yield centroids of clusters that can be used when labeling new data and labels for training data. Instead of having to waste your time setting group definitions before you actually take a look at the data, this clustering lets you find and analyze organically formed groups.

In machine learning, there is no one algorithm that works best for every problem you present it, particularly for supervised learning. The size and the structure of your dataset are several of the many different factors at play, meaning you should try out different algorithms to find one that is best suited to your problem. For example, when you clean your house, you have an array of different tools depending on what cleaning task you are attempting to accomplish: do you need a broom to sweep? Or do you need a vacuum to clean the carpet? You would choose the best tool for the job, or in this case, the best algorithm for your dataset.

Chapter 6: Applying Machine Learning and Artificial Intelligence to Improve Your Business

Machine learning can grant great results, but you should ensure that the problem you want to solve is complex enough to warrant its use in the first place. If you can structure this, then that scenario turns out to be a set of rules to solve your problem correctly, you may want to rethink the use of machine learning.

Some examples of machine learning already being used in well-established businesses include face detection, email spam filters, sales recommendations, speech recognition, real-time interactions, and fraud detection—some of which we touched on in earlier chapters regarding real-world applications.

As you can imagine it is difficult to train a computer to follow a set of rules that would allow them to detect and correctly identify an individual's face; think of all the physical differences between humans: skin colors, hair texture, eye color, etc. Like the algorithm Facebook uses that allows you to detect faces to tag, other algorithms can be trained to do the same. We all encounter spam, and some of us even take the time to mark the email as spam or edit the settings that determine that what comes into our inbox gets sent the right place. Much of the email spam filtering is put into context based on what content is relevant to each specific user, meaning what is relevant to Jane's inbox may not be relevant to Joe's inbox. A great supervised learning problem could be the receiving of a large email volume and have users go through them and marking what they consider to be spam.

Sales and product recommendations also come from someone's preferences, and our preferences all differ and are ever-changing. If you use Hulu or Netflix for example, both of those services have a section on their platform that suggests movies or TV shows they think you would like to watch based on anything you've ever watched while using the platform. Speech recognition, similar to face detection, can also be difficult based on the range of human speech from individual pronunciation to patterns of speech. Techemergence.com says "There is no single combination of sounds to specifically signal human speech...." Machine learning can identify patterns of speech and help convert speech to text.

Real-time interactions, like in online advertising, for example, would be hard to write strict rules for, say, to determine what kind of ad should pop up for a given user so that they are more likely to click on it. Facebook and Google use these kinds of algorithms, and machine learning can help us find patterns among user behavior and choose which individual ad is most likely to be relevant to which individual user. Fraud detection, like in the case of credit card purchases, only make up a small portion of fraud detection algorithms that can use solid rules. Since those attempting to commit fraud are constantly creating new ways to deceive us, these machine learning systems must be able, in real-time, to detect these patterns and determine commonalities between them and associate that with fraud.

What is the best kind of data to use with machine learning? "Clean data is better than big data," writes techemergence.com.

"If you have reams of business data from years ago, it may have no relevance today, particularly in fields where the basic business processes change drastically over the years, such as mobile e-commerce. If you have reams of unstructured and disjointed data, you may have too much 'cleaning' to do before you can ever get around to learning from the information collected."

Does your answer need to be very precise, or can you allow for some margin of error? We all can gain skill by practicing, adapting, growing, and improving through experiencing. In the same way, machine learning solutions can sometimes give incorrect answers a particular percentage of the time, particularly if you have recently fed it new or varied variables and information.

All in all, whether or not you decide to employ machine learning should come down to whether your problem is an actual priority or whether it's just something you want to play around with. If you, your company, or your team want to try out machine learning because you are interested or enthusiastic about it, there will be no real motivation behind your work and you will be less likely to commit to deriving an actual result. Don't just expect to build a machine-learning-based solution your first time through. Creating a successful algorithm is based on selecting the right kind of data, cleaning out that data to ensure source relevancy, and testing the data in a real environment while being ready to evaluate and make changes along the way.

Whether you are on a budget or you have a large company backing your foray into machine learning, you can start the incorporation of machine learning concepts into your business on a small scale using ready-made solutions. Here are seven examples below as written on Forbes.com:

1. Leveraging existing platforms

   "Building your own AI is unavoidably complex and expensive—but that doesn't mean it can't benefit you. Large companies like Google (Tensorflow) and Facebook (Fasttext) have open-sourced their own AI efforts, making it possible to build advanced AI into your own applications for a fraction of the cost."

2. Go one step at a time, beginning with productivity and client experience

   "You're not going to achieve AI-enablement overnight. Start small by integrating first-party apps that facilitate workforce productivity and predictive client experiences. When you're ready, cloud systems, open-sourced AI, and flexible workforce models all make for cost-effective AI development and infrastructure."

3. Tackle a small problem with high return on investment (ROI) potential

   "Start with a small problem with a high chance of demonstrating a positive return on investment (ROI). The key to success is these three steps: define, measure, decide. Define clear expectations and know what AI cannot do. Measure against meaningful baselines in your

AI experiment. Then decide whether the experiment worked or not."

4. Offer personalized content for customers

"We know AI is emerging and everyone wants to do something, but most businesses don't know where to start. I suggest businesses use AI to create personalized follow-up content to subscribers and customers based on their engagement with the business, along with interactions they have with initial email campaigns or website content like blog posts. This can be cost-effective."

5. Use artificial intelligence for analytics

"Artificial intelligence is far broader than what people typically think of when they hear AI. Analytics engines are a gateway true business AI. If you're trying to get into AI without investing heavily in machine learning, analytics software will help get your business intelligence at a bargain price."

6. Implement chatbots

"A good place to receive immediate value and ROI from AI is through chatbots. Their ability to interact with customers, answer basic questions and route inquiries appropriately allow companies with limited staff to seem much larger and improve customer service—even providing 24/7 call center support when it would be impossible to hire enough people to do this."

7. Automate the machine learning process

"Automating the machine learning process using open source tools can reduce the cost of implementing ML. Since 80% of the time is spent preparing the data, a tool that uses a graphical interface to transform, blend, and cleanse data can enable analysts to prepare the data in a self-service fashion without the need to rely on coding or scripting by developers or information technology (IT) operations."

Written by Erik Brynjolfsson and Andrew McAfee for The Harvard Business Review, The Business of Artificial Intelligence: What It Can—and Cannot—Do for Your Organization is an excellent article that covers the history of artificial intelligence and machine learning since the start of the field through its current updates. This article will help us explain the progression of artificial intelligence and how you can use the latest features in your business. We will begin where artificial intelligence has made the quickest advances: in the broad areas of perception and cognition.

"In the former category, some of the most practical advances have been made in relation to speech. Voice recognition is still far from perfect, but millions of people are now using it—think Siri, Alexa, and Google Assistant.... A study by the Stanford computer scientist James Landay and colleagues found that speech recognition is now about three times as fast, on average, as typing on a cell phone. The error rate, once 8.5%, has dropped to 4.9%. What's striking is that this substantial improvement has come not over the past 10 years but just since the summer of 2016."

Image recognition has drastically improved as well, though not as rapidly as the improvements that have been made regarding speech. "The speed of improvement has accelerated rapidly in recent years as a new approach, based on very large or "deep" neural nets, was adopted. The ML approach for vision systems is still far from flawless—but even people have trouble quickly recognizing puppies' faces or, more embarrassingly, see their cute faces where none exist."

We have been able to, over the years, create machine learning systems that can beat the best of the best players out there for games like chess and poker. These new machine learning systems not only replace the original algorithms but, in some cases, they are more superior relating to the task at hand than a human is at this time. While artificial intelligence systems have a limited scope of applicability, systems are being worked on that can exhibit general forms of intelligence across a wide array of domains instead of only being trained to complete certain tasks.

Next, we will take a more in-depth look at more complex machine learning systems you can incorporate into your business, starting with the analyzation of sales data. The way we look at sales growth has changed over the years thanks to the growing presence of digital interaction. Using data pulled from social media platforms and website visits, sales analysts no longer have to sift through this data in order to find necessary insights- they can now allow machine learning to take over these tasks.

Business has been looking to engage prospects and customers using a more personalized process and attempt to enhance their overall experience with your company so they will turn into repeat customers and continue to come back and buy your products again and again. Those who market on mobile channels or who develop applications are always on the lookout for all the leverage and information they can find about their customers to put it into some kind of context to be able to develop personalized experiences to the consumer that hopefully, in return, will yield to higher sales and profits.

Online shopping has grown exponentially in the last decade, and many shoppers now prefer to conduct their shopping online due to the speed, simplicity, and ability to view and compare options in real-time. The increase in online shoppers has caused criminals to target their fraud attempts online as well. Businesses do their best to stop fraud by enacting security measures but criminals are also out there attempting to break through those measures at every turn. While these measures are for the shopper's safety, they may annoy the shopper by slowing down the transaction times and overall purchase experience, sometimes resulting in a negative impact on the brand's image.

Some people find personalized recommendations endearing, while others wonder how Facebook knew you were thinking about buying new rims for your car because all of the ads you are seeing while on their platform are pertaining to car rims. Even in-store, customers usually will enjoy it when they are approached by a sales team member who can direct them to what part of the store they should search in based on the item they are looking for, or if in a retail setting they can help you narrow down your choices for a new t-shirt. Amazon was one of the first businesses to use an algorithm to improve this recommendation process, but since then, other machine learning systems have become much more successful. By having the system leverage machine learning and use analytics that can predict outcomes, a brand can search beyond what the customer is looking for and begin to see a broader pattern on what a customer might like to see in future ads.

Learning management systems (LMS) bring great value to business through ongoing eLearning opportunities across all segments. eLearningIndustry.com writes, "the most significant role that Machine Learning plays in eLearning is personalization. This is achieved through more effective data analysis and automation. An LMS that uses Machine Learning is able to access user data and use it to improve the eLearning experience. However, it can also be fully integrated with your HR systems to analyze learner data and pinpoint trends with greater efficiency. This allows you to identify areas for improvement based on analytical patterns and pre-set algorithms." Employee retention and satisfaction can also be improved through the combination of human resources and LMS. "Predictive analytics and iterative evaluations allow you to pinpoint patterns, such as a significant spike in course drop-outs or certification lapses. Thus, you can intervene before it's too late to retain your top talent and ensure that everyone is in compliance, saving you the expense of having to vet job candidates and retrain new hires." A variety of other uses for Machine Learning in eLearning are automated online training paths, adaptable online training resources, targeted recommendations, improvement of resource allocation, more efficient online assessment strategies, and intuitive planning and development.

Dynamic pricing is behind the success of sites that allow you to book a hotel like Priceline or Hotwire; the systems used by these businesses can change the pricing of a hotel room based on the need or perceived level of demand. UBER and Airbnb are another two platforms that use dynamic pricing in their business model. UBER also uses the systems to cut down on user wait times and optimize carpooling through their new rideshare features. Machine learning is able to leverage this existing data into a prediction of where the next demand is most likely to occur.

Lastly, natural language processing (NLP) has an abundance of functions that could be helped along regarding tedious tasks. Technical support, help desks, customer service, and other functions benefit from machine learning's capability to have a computer take of NLP. Automated translation methods between humans and computers are provided by NLP, and machine learning focuses on the nuances of the human language like out word choice, the context of what we said, what we meant to say, and our growing usage of slang and jargon. Chatbot usage has grown and these algorithms allow for the replacement of humans in certain situations and communication can continue to happen even if complex information is involved.

Machine learning and trading

Regarding the business of trading, machine learning has far-reaching possibilities, and in this section of the book, we will walk you through the creation of a trading strategy plan. You can take one of two approaches to setting up this strategy, and that is to make the strategy model-based or to use data mining. Model-based strategies use inefficient market models and then construct representations mathematically and then test their long-term validity. If you used a data mining approach, patterns become important because only those that are identified will continue to repeat in future system cycles.

So what is the overall impact of machine learning on trading you ask? Slow progress has been taking place, like the few hedge funds that are very active in the field, due to a low acceptance of the technology mainly involving its investment costs into new tools and talent. According to towardsdatascience.com, "the majority of funds use fundamental analysis because this is what managers learn in their MBA programs. There are not many hedge funds that rely solely on AI. Application of AI is growing at the retail level but the majority of traders still use methods that were proposed in mid-twentieth century, including traditional technical analysis, because they are easy to learn and apply." Applications for artificial intelligence will continue to change along with every other technological advancement, meaning current and future traders must become familiar with the technology to find a good mix between the old ways of providing financial advice and the new method of using algorithms to teach a system to do these things on its own.

Here at the steps to create your own trading strategy:

1. Setting up the problem
2. Collecting reliable data
3. Spitting the data
4. Feature engineering
5. Selecting a model
6. Train, validate, and optimize
7. Backtest on the test data

Setting up the problem

Start off by asking yourself: what do you want to predict? What makes a good prediction? How will I evaluate my methods and the outcome? Once we know our target value, deciding on the method to evaluate your predictions will come next, and you will need to try out different models to find one that is the best fit for your data.

Collecting reliable data

"You need to think about what data will have predictive power for the target variable Y—if we were predicting Price, you could use Stock Price Data, Stock Trade Volume Data, Fundamental Data, Price and Volume Data of Correlated stocks, an Overall Market indicator like Stock Index Level, Price of other correlated assets, etc. You will need to setup data access for this data, and make sure your data is accurate, free of errors and solve for missing data (quite common)," states Medium.com. "Also ensure your data is unbiased and adequately represents all market conditions (example equal number of winning and losing scenarios) to avoid bias in your model. You may also need to clean your data for dividends, stock splits, rolls etc."

Spitting the data

This is one of the most important steps because we need to separate groups of data in order to train our system: we need training data and testing data, so we recommend a 60/70% training split and 30/40% test split. "Since training data is used to evaluate model parameters, your model will likely be overfitted to training data and training data metrics will be misleading about model performance. If you do not keep any separate test data and use all your data to train, you will not know how well or badly your model performs on new unseen data. *This is one of the major reasons why well-trained ML models fail on live data—* people train on all available data and get excited by training data metrics, but the model fails to make any meaningful predictions on live data that it wasn't trained on."

However, there is a problem with this method due to the fact that if we are training on the same data over and over, we are unable to evaluate the performance of our model, therefore unable to guarantee a good prediction from new data it receives. "To solve for this we can create a separate validation data set. Now you can train on training data, evaluate performance on validation data, optimize until you are happy with the performance, and finally test on test data. This way, the test data stays untainted and we don't use any information from test data to improve our model." Remember that once you have performed a check on the test data that you will not go back and continue to optimize the model any further.

Feature engineering

"Now comes the real engineering. The golden rule of feature selection is that the predictive power should come from primarily from the features and not from the model. You will find that the choice of features has a far greater impact on performance than the choice of model." Some suggestions for choosing features include exploring the relationship between the set of features and the target variable and choosing features that have a relationship to the target variable. "ML models tend to perform well with normalization. However, normalization is tricky when working with time series data because the future range of data is unknown. Your data could fall out of bounds of your normalization leading to model errors."

Selecting a model

The way the problem is framed will affect which model you choose to use when solving your problem. We suggest researching the math behind all of the different model options to ensure the best fit.

Train, validate, and optimize

Your model will be trained using the training data, and its performance will be measured based on validation data. After measuring the success or failure, you will go back and make changes so that the system can re-train and you can then re-evaluate it. If you are not happy with the outcome you can always backtrack a few steps and choose another model that may work better.

Backtest on the test data

At this step, you will be running your final model version using the test data that we set aside at the start and have not yet used. "This provides you with a realistic expectation of how your model is expected to perform on new and unseen data when you start trading live. Hence, it is necessary to ensure you have a clean dataset that you haven't used to train or validate your model." At this point in the game, if you do not like the results, do not go back and try to re-optimize. Your next step should be to create a new set of test data and choose another model to use.

Conclusion

Thank you for making it through to the end of *Machine Learning Guide: A Practical Approach for Businesses*, let's hope it was informative and able to provide you with all of the tools you need to achieve your goals whatever they may be. We hope that after reading this book you have an overall better grasp of what artificial intelligence is and how it relates to deep learning, neural networks, and machine learning.

The Harvard Business Review has stated that "the most important general-purpose technology of our era is artificial intelligence, particularly machine learning (ML)—that is, the machine's ability to keep improving its performance without humans having to explain exactly how to accomplish all the tasks it's given. Within just the past few years machine learning has become far more effective and widely available. We can now build systems that learn how to perform tasks on their own."

We have yet to see all of the ways artificial intelligence can impact our lives and our businesses; in fact, some of the biggest opportunities in the field have yet to be tapped into. "The effects of AI will be magnified in the coming decade, as manufacturing, retailing, transportation, finance, healthcare, law, advertising, insurance, entertainment, education, and virtually every other industry transform their core processes and business models to take advantage of machine learning. The bottleneck now is in management, implementation, and business imagination."

There is good news out there involving organizations that are looking to incorporate machine learning into their daily operations or strategic plans for down the road. Artificial intelligence skillsets are quickly spreading thanks to online resources like those at Udacity and Coursera that offer intelligent and motivate students, or really people of any age, an opportunity to learn basic introductory artificial intelligence concepts. Some will get to the point in their learning that they are able to create their own high-level machine learning systems. Other good news is "that the necessary algorithms and hardware for modern AI can be bought or rented as needed," according to the Harvard Business Review. Lastly, people greatly overestimate the amount of data needed to start making use of a machine learning system. If you are only looking to significantly improve your organization's functionality and your goal is not to dominate the global market, a smaller set of data is easy to find and use in your computations.

"Machine learning is driving changes at three levels: tasks and occupations, business processes, and business models. An example of task-and-occupation redesign is the use of machine vision systems to identify potential cancer cells—freeing up radiologists to focus on truly critical cases, to communicate with patients, and to coordinate with other physicians." You would be hard-pressed to find a system that can completely replace a job worked by a human. Most often they complement the job and make the work more valuable instead of impeding the progress. "Does that mean there is no limit to what artificial intelligence and machine learning can do? Perception and cognition cover a great deal of territory—from driving a car to forecasting sales to deciding whom to hire or promote. We believe the chances are excellent that AI will soon reach superhuman levels of performance in most or all of these areas." So what are you waiting for? Go out and explore all that AI has to offer today!

Finally, if you found this book useful in any way, a review on Amazon is always appreciated!